Weather round the world

Wherever we live in the world the
weather influences our lives.
Sun, rain, wind and snow affect the
houses we build, the foods we can grow,
what we wear and what we do each
day. Some people say that the weather
also affects our health and our moods.

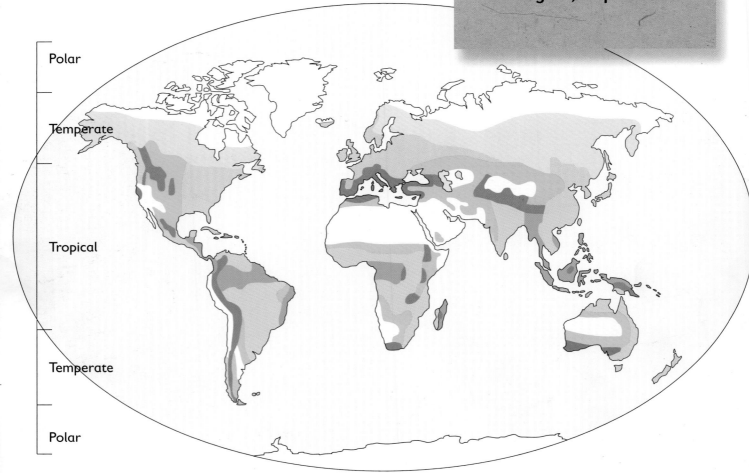

Polar

Temperate

Tropical

Temperate

Polar

Three main climate zones:

■	Tropical:	Hot and wet for most of the year.
■	Temperate:	Mild and rainy; four separate seasons.
□	Polar:	Very cold for most of the year.

Smaller climate zones:

■	Subtropical:	Hot, fairly wet, but long dry season.
□	Arid:	Very dry; hot in daytime, cold at night.
■	Semi-arid:	Hot days, cool nights, fairly dry.
■	Mediterranean:	Hot, dry summers; cool wet winters.
□	Northern temperate:	Mild summers, cold, long, rainy winters.
■	Mountain:	Cold and snowy.

Climate zones

There are three main climate zones in the world: tropical (hot and wet), temperate (mild and rainy), polar (cold and snowy).

The weather within these main zones can vary a lot, especially where there are mountains, or where land is beside the sea. Because of this, there are smaller climate zones within the three main zones.

◀ *You can see the main climate zones and the smaller climate zones on this map.*

Weather words

Many different words are used to describe weather. Some weather words are listed below. See if you can find them and discover what they mean as you read through this book:

climate

meteorologist

satellite

temperature

cumulus

forecast

tornado

El Niño

Try This! Weather zones

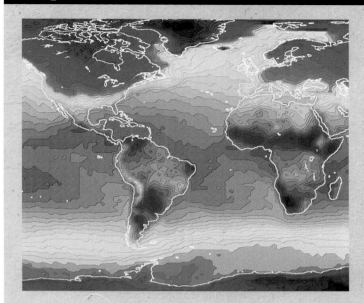

◀ *This satellite picture of earth, taken from space, is coloured according to temperature. Red and deep red show the hottest areas; pink shows the next hottest area, then yellow. Warm oceans are shown as light blue; cold oceans are dark blue.*

Use this photograph and the world map (*see page 4*) to create your own picture of the world's climate zones.

Instead of using different colours to show the different temperatures of each zone, you could draw people wearing the most appropriate clothing for the zone they are in. For example, if you were in a polar climate, you would need to be wrapped up very warm.

Or you could make up a key for each zone like the weather symbols you see on the weather forecast.

Very hot, very cold

The world's weather can range from very hot to very cold. The temperature – indicating how hot it is in an area – is measured with a thermometer. It is usually measured in one of two units – Fahrenheit or Celsius.

Fahrenheit and Celsius

In 1714, the German scientist Gabriel Fahrenheit developed a scale for measuring temperature. He based it on two things that he had noticed: the freezing point and the boiling point of water. He called the freezing point of water 32°F and the boiling point 212°F.

In 1742, the Swedish astronomer Anders Celsius invented a new scale. This was improved five years later by the Swedish scientist, Carolus Linnaeus. The Celsius scale is based on the freezing point of water being 0°C and boiling point of water being 100°C.

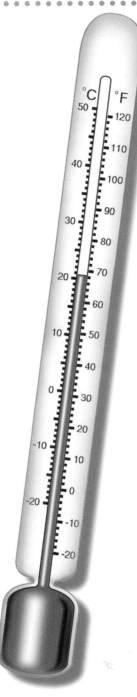

▲ Mathematicians and scientists found the Celsius, or Centigrade, scale much easier to use than the Fahrenheit scale.

Number work

Use the thermometer on this page to help work out these problems. You can give your answers in °C or °F.

✪ What is the difference between the world's hottest average temperature of 34.4°C (94°F) and the world's coldest average temperature of -57.8°C (-72°F).

✪ What is the difference between the highest temperature ever recorded 57.8°C (136°F) and the lowest temperature ever recorded -89.2°C (-128.6°F)?

✪ Make up some more temperature puzzles of your own and give them to a friend to solve.

Did you know...

The highest temperature ever recorded on earth was 57.8°C (136°F) in Libya, North Africa.

The country with the hottest weather all year round is Ethiopia, also in Africa. The average temperature there is 34.4°C (94°F).

The coldest temperature ever measured was -89.2°C (-128.6°F) in Antarctica.

Antarctica is also the coldest continent all year round. The average temperature there is -57.8°C (-72°F).

◆ *It is very difficult to grow crops in the hot, dry climate of Ethiopia.*

◆ *Antarctica is one of the windiest, as well as coldest, places on earth.*

Feeling the heat

People have learnt how to live in many different environments, but we can suffer if temperatures rise or fall too much.

At around 32°C (90°F) people start to feel very hot and sticky. At 41°C (105°F) we begin to feel unwell. Temperatures above this can be dangerous because the body starts to overheat.

We also suffer at low temperatures. Without clothes, we feel cold at 20°C (68°F).

Temperature is affected by the wind. We feel colder if the wind is blowing.

Keeping hot, keeping cold

Materials that don't allow heat to pass through are called insulators. Insulators protect our bodies from losing heat and from becoming too cold.

This experiment will help you find out which materials are the best insulators, and why.

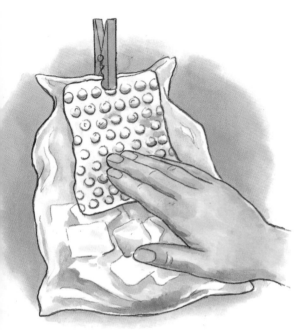

Insulators Part One

You will need:

- plastic bag filled with ice
- clothes peg
- hot water bottle (get an adult to help you with this)
- pen and paper

ASK AN ADULT

- piece of aluminium foil
- paper
- cotton wool pad
- piece of plastic bubble wrap
- cotton garment, eg a blouse
- woollen garment, eg a jumper

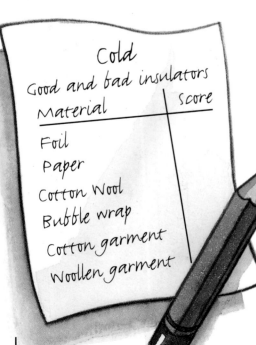

Cold
Good and bad insulators
Material   score
Foil
Paper
Cotton Wool
Bubble wrap
Cotton garment
Woollen garment

1 Use the clothes peg to attach the different materials to the plastic bag as shown.

2 Gently touch each item in turn.

3 Which feels the coldest?

Give each material a score out of 10. Give 10 for most cold; 1 for least cold.

4 Write down your scores in a chart (see left).

If you can feel the cold through the material it is not a good insulator. It is allowing the heat from your hand to pass through to the ice in the bag.

Insulators Part Two

1 *Repeat the experiment using the hot water bottle instead of the bag of ice.*

2 *Give each material a score. Give 10 for the most heat you can feel through the material and 1 for the least heat.*

3 *Write down your scores in a chart.*

The materials that let through the least heat are the best insulators. Put the materials in order, listing them from the best insulator (lowest number) to the worst insulator (highest number).

? **Look closely at your lowest-scoring materials. What are they like?**

You will probably find that the plastic bubble wrap and the jumper worked best as insulators. This is because they both trap air between their layers. Air is a very good insulator.

Trapped Air

Skin

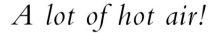

Material

▶ *Wearing many layers of clothes allows people to survive in temperatures as low as -60°C (-76°F).*

A lot of hot air!

The right clothes can insulate people from the dangerous effect of extreme heat or cold. In hot climates people wear long, loose clothes which leave room for air to circulate inside. In cold climates people wear many layers of clothes which trap air in between the layers and keep in the body heat.

The changing seasons

In many parts of the world the weather patterns change several times in a year. These regular weather patterns are called seasons.

We expect the weather to behave in certain ways in each season.

Winter is the coldest season; summer is the hottest. Spring and autumn are usually somewhere in between.

Try This! Sunflakes

If sunlight fell like snowflakes,
gleaming yellow and so bright,
we could build a sunman,
we could have a sunman fight,
we could watch the sunflakes
drifting in the sky.

We could go sleighing...
through sundrifts and sunbanks,
we could ride a sunmobile,
and we could touch sunflakes –
I wonder how they'd feel.

FRANK ASCH

Try writing a poem about other weather in this way, such as fog flakes or snow beams.

Winter is the coldest season. Days are often wet and foggy. There is sometimes snow and ice.

Spring can be wet and windy, with some warmer, sunny days.

Summer is the hottest season. But there can be thunderstorms and heavy rain, as well as hot, sunny days.

Autumn can bring frosty mornings, with cooler days and nights. The days can be sunny, but not always hot.

The reason for seasons

Seasons occur because of the way the earth orbits (moves round) the sun.

The earth is tilted at an angle: different parts of the earth get different amounts of heat and light at different times of the year.

As the earth moves around the sun, the part tilted towards the sun gets more heat and light from the sun's rays. It has summer.

The part tilted away from the sun gets less heat and light, and so it has winter.

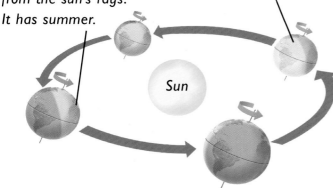

Sun

Season festivals

People around the world celebrate the changing seasons in different ways.

◀ *In India, men dance and play music in the street as part of the spring festival.*

◀ *A masked dancer at an autumn festival in Tibet.*

Weather forecasts

In the past there were no scientific weather forecasts, but people still needed to know what weather conditions to expect. Like today, farmers needed to know when the weather would be fine so they could sow or harvest their crops. Sailors wanted to steer clear of dangerous storms at sea.

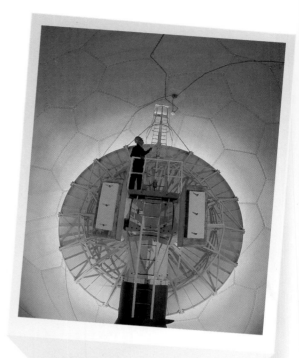

This weather radar helps to make modern weather forecasts much more accurate than forecasts in the past.

Try This!

Be a natural weather forecaster. Test these old-fashioned ways of foretelling the weather to find out if they work.

Find a pine cone or (if you can get to the seaside) a strip of seaweed. Hang either up out of doors, in a sheltered place.

When the air is moist (a sign of approaching rain) the pine cone will close up and the seaweed will feel limp and slimy.

When the air is dry (a sign of fine weather), the pine cone will open and the seaweed will feel stiff and leathery.

Weather-watchers

Today, scientists called meteorologists study the weather. They use radar to monitor rain and snow. Weather balloons and satellites give us information about clouds and storms. All this information is automatically radioed to weather stations on the ground.

At the weather stations meteorologists analyse the information to help them to predict weather patterns. However, they don't always get it right!

Did you know...

Weather balloons carry instruments that take temperature readings high above the earth.

Radar is a system for finding the positions of objects in the air. Heavy rain, thunderstorms, hurricanes and tornadoes show up on radar. It sends out radio waves which bounce back off clouds or storms.

Weather satellites orbit the earth. They send back pictures of how clouds are forming.

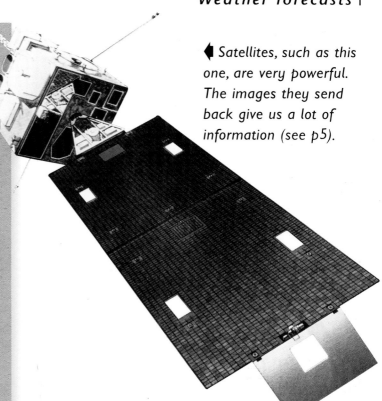

◀ *Satellites, such as this one, are very powerful. The images they send back give us a lot of information (see p5).*

Weather sayings

Before modern technology, people learnt to predict weather patterns by watching nature.

They made up sayings to help them remember what they had found out.

*A sunshiny shower
Won't last an hour.*

*Clear moon,
Frost soon.*

◀ *Some sayings are true. A cold, frosty morning often follows a bright, clear moonlit night. But when the moon is surrounded by clouds, damp, stormy weather often follows the next day.*

Clouds

The air around us contains water, although we cannot usually see it. This water comes from the sea, rivers and lakes.

When the sun heats up water on the surface of the sea, rivers and lakes, it evaporates and turns into a gas called water vapour. In the air, the water vapour joins together and becomes tiny droplets of water.

The clouds we see floating in the sky are made of these water droplets. When clouds rise very high above the earth's surface, they cool down and the water droplets turn into crystals of ice.

Clouds form in many different shapes and sizes.

➡ *Different clouds are often linked to different types of weather.*

Cirrus clouds form high in the sky, where it is coldest.

Delicate alto-cumulus clouds are signs of approaching gales.

Stratus clouds are large, low clouds that often lead to drizzle.

Huge cumulo-nimbus clouds bring thunderstorms.

▶ *Meteorologists can tell a lot by studying the formation of clouds.*

THE CLOUD MOBILE

Do you know what the poem is describing?
Look at this picture to help you work it out.

Above my face is a map.
Continents form and fade.
Blue countries, made
on a white sea, are erased,
and white countries traced
on a blue sea.

MAY SWENSON

Try This! Make a cloud mobile

You will need:
white card
white or clear thread
sticky tape
black colouring pencil
lengths of plastic tube or bamboo

YOU CAN TRY THIS!

1 Using the pictures on these pages to help you, draw and cut out the different types of clouds. Shade the dark clouds with the black colouring pencil.

2 Fix lengths of thread to each of your cut-outs with tape.

3 Hang each cloud from a different length of wire. Use the picture on page 14 to get each different type of cloud at the right height.

4 Attach the clouds onto a plastic tube or bamboo to make a mobile. You will have to move the thread on the tube or bamboo to make it balance.

▲ *Hang your mobile where the clouds have plenty of room to move.*

15

Rain

Did you know...

The largest amount of rainfall recorded in one day was 1,869.9 mm at Réunion, an island in the Indian Ocean.

The largest amount of rainfall recorded in one year was 26,461.7 mm at Cherrapunji, India.

The driest place in the world is the Atacama Desert in South America. It gets less than 0.08 mm of rainfall a year.

▲ These people in Ethiopia gather to watch flood waters rage past their village, after two years of drought.

Over the centuries rain has been welcomed and feared. It has brought life-giving water to people, animals and plants. It has also caused terrible floods, sweeping away houses, covering roads and ruining crops in waterlogged fields.

Rain forms when tiny water droplets in clouds combine and make bigger, heavier drops that fall to the ground.

Different types of cloud produce different types of rainfall. Flat sheets of stratus clouds (*see page 14*), which cover a wide area, produce long periods of rain. Fluffy-looking cumulus clouds, which are surrounded by blue sky, produce short showers.

Rainmakers

Throughout history, people have held special ceremonies and said prayers to try to make rain fall.

In medieval Europe witches threatened to create storms against people who annoyed them. They claimed to have wind and rain tied up in their handkerchiefs.

In ancient America the Hopi people held rain dances to try to end droughts.

Native Americans living on the Great Plains prayed to the Thunderbird who brought rain.

Make a rain measure

1   Cut the top off the bottle.

2   Use a waterproof pen and ruler to mark centimetres and millimetres up the side of the bottle.

3   Place the cut-off bottle top upside down over the main part of the bottle, to make a funnel.

4   Place the bottle on a flat piece of ground away from overhanging buildings or trees.

5   Observe the rainwater level every day; record it in your notebook, then pour the rainwater away.

You will need:
- plastic bottle
- scissors
- waterproof pen
- ruler
- notebook and pen

Try to keep rainfall records every day for a month. You could record your findings as a bar chart. Choose the week in which you had the most rain. Put the days of the week along the bottom axis of the bar chart. Put millimetres and centimetres along the upright side of the chart. Draw in your results for that week (see the chart to the left to help you).

  Did it rain every day? Which was the wettest day? How much rain fell?

Thunder and lightning

Thunderstorms can happen anytime, and anywhere except Antarctica (where it is too cold). They occur most often in spring and summer, and in tropical regions (see *map, page 4*).

Electricity

Thunderstorms are caused by huge masses of warm air collecting together in a cloud, and rising high into the sky. The air inside the thundercloud rises and falls. Vast amounts of electricity build up inside it. No one knows quite how this happens.

Electricity inside thunderclouds causes the air to expand (get larger) and make a booming sound, called thunder.

Electricity that jumps across thunderclouds or to the ground is known as lightning.

Did you know...

Lightning travels amazingly fast – about 96,000 kilometres per second.

It is also amazingly hot – over 22,000°C (40,000°F).

An average thunderstorm lasts for about 15 minutes, though it can last for up to 2 hours.

There are about 40,000 thunderstorms worldwide every day.

Some thunderclouds are so big that they can be seen from over 320 km away.

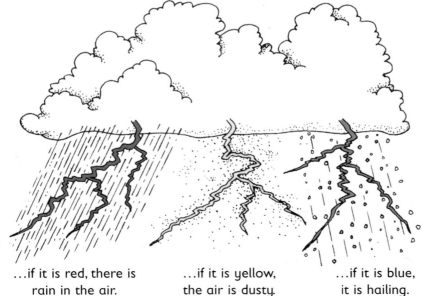

...if it is red, there is rain in the air.

...if it is yellow, the air is dusty.

...if it is blue, it is hailing.

◀ *Lightning can be several different colours, depending on the air it travels through. If the lightning is white, then the air is dry…*

Keep safe in a storm

Move indoors if possible, or get inside a car or a bus.

Do not touch electrical equipment (including telephones and computers) or water pipes.

If outdoors, stay away from anything metal, like gates or fences.

Do not shelter under lamp posts, signposts or trees.

⚠ **BEWARE** If your hair stands on end, this means danger! Crouch close to the ground.

Do not look up, or lie flat, until the storm has passed.

⬆ *Cloud-to-ground lightning causes fires, and can strike people.*

Wordgame

Can you make at least 50 words from the letters in:

T h u n d e r s t o r m

Here are some to start you off: thunder, storm, store, under, mother, drum...

THOR AND THE MIDGARD SERPENT

According to ancient Viking legends, Thor, the god of thunder, rode through the sky in a chariot pulled by goats, smashing giant snakes with his mighty hammer and creating thunder and lightning. Thor was the favourite god of Viking peasants and farmers.

The Vikings lived their lives by the sea and were fearless sailors. They believed that the sea and waves were ruled by different gods. But violent storms at sea were caused by a huge and evil serpent – the serpent of Midgard. It lay beneath the waves and curled its enormous body around the world.

Thor hated the serpent. He was determined to kill it. He asked the giant fishermen, who knew where it lived, for help. One of the giants, Hymir, agreed.

Thor and Hymir set off in a small boat with an ox's head as bait. They reached the place where they believed the serpent to be. Thor fixed the ox's head to a giant hook attached to a thick, strong rope. He launched them into the sea and waited.

Suddenly the rope tightened; the sea turned black and began to churn. Thor quickly took up the rope. He pulled with all his strength, and as he pulled the serpent's head rose from the stormy waves.

The serpent of Midgard, hooked by the tongue, realised the power of Thor. It wrapped its immense body around the rocks under the sea, but still it could not withstand Thor's great strength. As the tiring serpent fought, it spat its venom and flashed its fierce eyes.

Hymir, frightened and not realising the serpent was weakening, could bear it no longer. He struck the rope with his axe. Thor fell back. The serpent sank below the waves before Thor could throw his hammer.

Thor could not believe what Hymir had done. In his rage, Thor cast Hymir into the depths of the sea.

The serpent recovered from its wounds. The Vikings believed that it continued to stir up stormy seas, causing many of their ships to be wrecked.

Wild winds

Wind is moving air. Air moves because it is hotter or colder, wetter or drier, than other air nearby.

World winds

Many different types of wind blow over the surface of the earth. You can see two of the most important ones in the diagrams below.

Some winds feel wild and strong; others feel soft and gentle. Many winds blow in the same areas at the same time every year. They are so well-known that they have names.

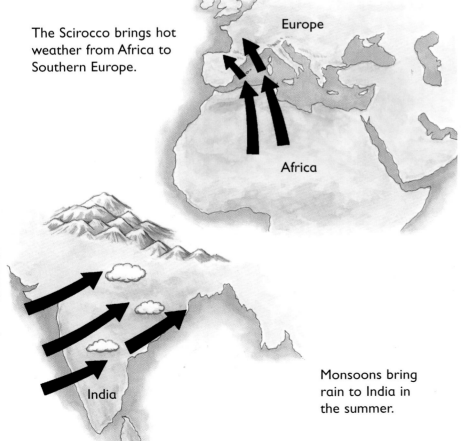

The Scirocco brings hot weather from Africa to Southern Europe.

Europe

Africa

India

Monsoons bring rain to India in the summer.

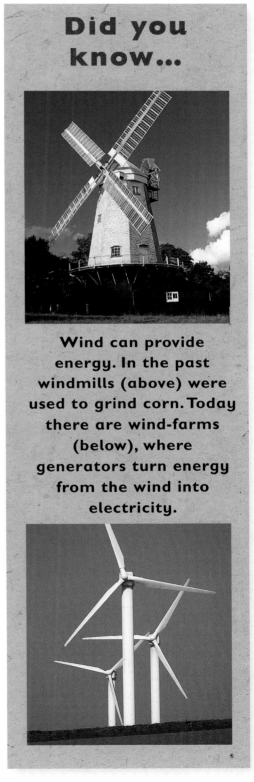

Swirling storms

In hot, tropical regions, several large thunderstorms sometimes bunch together over the ocean. The massive clouds they contain swirl round and round. They form a huge wall, up to 15 km high, around an area of calm in the centre.

These swirling clouds begin to move across the ocean, getting faster all the time. They produce winds of more than 250 kph. They create enormous amounts of rain – up to 600 mm in one day. They cause massive waves called 'storm surges'.

◀ *This swirling storm, shown in black with the area of calm at the centre in white, is moving across the United States (left and below).*

▶ *This type of swirling storm is called a typhoon, cyclone or hurricane in different parts of the world.*

Did you know...

Tornadoes are terrifying funnel-shaped storms. They are one of the most dangerous types of weather. Tornadoes are formed when thunder-clouds meet high-speed winds many kilometres above ground. Tall, twisting columns of air form inside the cloud, and spin down to the ground. This causes a fierce whirlwind, rushing round and round at almost 500 kph. It can snatch up heavy objects, such as cars, and can tear the roofs off buildings.

Snow and ice

Snow and ice are formed when water vapour in clouds falls to a temperature of 0°C (32°F) or below. Then the water vapour turns into crystals of ice. The ice crystals join together and become too heavy to float in the air. They fall to the ground as snowflakes.

▶ *Snowflakes are made up of ice crystals. The crystals combine to make beautiful patterns.*

⬆ *These larger-than-life figures in Sapporo, Japan, are sculpted out of snow.*

Dangerous beauty

Ice and snow look very beautiful and can be great fun to play in. But they can also be dangerous. Ice on roads makes driving very difficult. Huge snowfalls in mountain areas can come crashing down the slopes as avalanches, covering the villages below.

Never walk on frozen ponds or lakes: ice may look thick, but it can break easily underfoot.

Snow sculptures

Every year in February, the Japanese city of Sapporo holds a huge Snow Festival. Artists carve enormous statues, many times larger than life, out of tightly packed snow.

Weather wonders

unlight, wind, water and ice can create many magical weather effects.

Rainbows

Rainbows appear in showery weather. They are made when sunlight shines on water droplets in the sky. Sunlight looks clear and white, but it is made up of many different colours. Each water droplet splits up the sunlight into the different colours of the rainbow.

➤ *Rainbows are curved. The lower the sun is in the sky, the higher the rainbow arch will be.*

Make a rainbow

Choose a sunny day for this experiment.

You will need:
- shallow bowl
- clean water
- small mirror
- white wall or big sheet of white paper

1 *Place the bowl close to a sunny window.*

2 *Half fill the bowl with water.*

3 *Hold the mirror at an angle in the water.*

4 *Use the mirror to reflect a beam of sunlight onto the sheet of paper or wall.*

5 *Gently move the mirror in the water until you see a patch of rainbow on the paper or wall.*

The sunlight travelling through the water has been split into all its separate colours.

Safety note: *Do not look directly at the sun or shine the reflected sunlight from the mirror into your eyes.*

Try This!

Frost only forms when the temperature falls below freezing (0°C or 32°F), and usually when the nights are clear and there is no cloud cover in the sky.

Many countries have a story character called Jack Frost who probably comes from Scandinavian myths. When the ground is covered in frost, it is said there has been a visit from Jack Frost himself.

What do you think Jack Frost would look like? You could draw a picture of him.

Frost

Frost can be as beautiful to look at as a rainbow. Frost is frozen dew. It is made up of tiny ice crystals that freeze into jewel-like patterns.

▲ *Thick frost is called hoar frost. It can be so thick that it looks like snow.*

Changing weather

The world began about 4.6 billion years ago. World climates and weather have changed throughout the centuries. In the past climates changed very gradually. But today scientists believe climates in all zones are changing more and more quickly. The whole world may be getting warmer.

Some scientists think that natural events may have caused these changes. They blame dust from volcanic eruptions and 'wobbles' in the earth's orbit around the sun (see p11).

▲ *Burning fuels cause pollution.*

(see p11)

Did you know...

El Niño is the name given to warm sea currents that flow into the usually cold Pacific Ocean, off the coast of Peru. These warm waters upset the normal temperatures in the air around the earth. They have an amazing knock-on effect on the world's weather. El Niño can cause floods in Australia, droughts in South Africa and can disturb weather patterns in Europe and North America.

El Niño means 'the Christ child' in Spanish: it was given this name because it happens at Christmas time.

Air pollution

Other scientists think that weather changes have been caused by people.

We need a lot of energy to live our lives today. We burn fuel, such as oil and coal, to provide the energy needed to power cars, trucks, planes and ships. Factories, shops and power stations also burn many tonnes of fuel. Burning fuels gives off gases that pollute the air.

Trees naturally use up some of the gases that are given off when fuels are burned. But in some parts of the world large areas of trees are cut down every day to make room to grow crops, graze cattle or build houses.

Global warming

Scientists believe all these changes can cause global warming. This is the gradual build-up of heat within the earth's atmosphere. Global warming may be affecting our weather.

Scientists check both natural changes and levels of pollution all the time to see what effects they have on the world's weather.

➤ *Data is fed back continually from radars and satellites to this control room so meteorologists can monitor the weather.*

Try This! Weather record

You can monitor the weather in your area by starting a long-term weather diary. Record what the weather is like twice a day. Write down the temperature, whether it is sunny or cloudy (p14), or if it is raining (p17).

Include in your diary a section for recording what the weather forecast is. Note down the forecast in the evening. Compare it with the weather you actually record the following day.

Date	Forecast	Temp°C	Rainfall	Weather
am				
pm				

Look through the national newspapers every week to see if there are any reports of weather disasters. Look back at your long-term weather report and see if any major changes in your local weather happened at the same time as the weather disaster.

Better technology

With better and better technology, scientists can measure changes in the weather more accurately: spacecraft monitor the activity of the sun, specially equipped planes record data at the centre of hurricanes and floating weather stations gather information to try to predict such big changes in weather patterns as caused by the El Niño effect.

What's more...

More windy things

Wind speed can be measured in a number of ways: miles or kilometres per hour, or in knots (one knot is **1.85 kph**). Another way to measure wind speed is to use the Beaufort Scale. Sir Frances Beaufort was an admiral in the Royal Navy. He developed a system of measuring the force of wind for sailors to use. He divided wind speeds into **13 points**.

Beaufort Scale

Force	mph	kph	Description	Effects on land
0	1	1	calm	smoke rises straight into air
1	2-3	1-5	light	air rising; smoke drifts slowly
2	4-7	6-11	light breeze	smoke shows direction of wind
3	8-12	12-19	gentle breeze	leaves and twigs move
4	13-18	20-29	moderate breeze	small branches move; paper blows about
5	19-24	30-38	fresh breeze	small, leafy trees sway
6	25-31	39-51	strong breeze	difficult to use umbrellas; large branches sway
7	32-38	51-61	near gale	difficult to walk into wind
8	39-46	62-74	gale	twigs snap off trees
9	47-54	75-86	strong gale	branches break; slates blown off roofs
10	55-63	87-101	whole gale	trees uprooted
11	64-74	102-120	storm	cars overturned; trees blown some distance
12	over 74	over 120	hurricane	widespread destruction; buildings destroyed

Use the descriptions of the Beaufort Scale to draw a picture chart of each stage.

Weather music

If you can play the recorder, try playing this piece of music taken from Antonio Vivaldi's (1678–1741) 'The Four Seasons'.

Try This! Clothes for climates

You will need: • thin card • scissors • coloured pencils or pens • books showing people in different parts of the world

1 Cut the thin card into 24 pieces, about the same size and shape as playing cards.

2 Divide the cards into six sets of four cards, one set for the following climate zones: Mediterranean, polar, mountain, coastal, arid and tropical.

3 From your resource books find out as much as you can about the weather in these zones, and what people wear. You may like to work in a group, with each member finding out about a different climate zone.

4 Take one set of cards and decide which climate zone you will show.

5 Draw a head-covering suitable for that zone on one card, a suitable top or coat on another card, suitable trousers or a skirt on the third card, and something suitable to wear on the feet on the last card. Write the climate zone on each card. When you have four cards for each climate zone you are ready to play.

Get together with three or four friends. Collect all the cards and shuffle them. Share them out equally.

You need to collect as many sets of cards as you can. Take it in turns to ask the other players if they have a card from a particular climate zone. For example, 'Jo, do you have a top from a tropical zone?' If the player does have the card, they must give it to you and you can ask another question. If they do not have the card, that is the end of your turn.

The winner is the person who collects the most complete sets of cards.

mountain

Glossary

arid: dry. An arid climate is very dry, and usually hot in the daytime and cold at night.

atmosphere: the air that surrounds the earth.

average: a standard that is accepted as normal. For example, the average temperature of an area is the temperature that occurs most often in that area.

boiling point: the temperature at which a liquid turns into a gas. For example, water turns to water vapour at 100°C (212°F). This is the boiling point of water.

climate: the long-term weather pattern in a certain region or place.

combine: to join together.

continent: one of the six main land masses on the earth. These are Europe, Asia, Africa, North and South America, Australasia and Antarctica.

cyclone: a violent, whirling wind.

droplets: very tiny drops.

freezing point: the temperature at which a liquid turns into a solid. For example, water turns to ice at 0°C (32°F). This is the freezing point of water.

generator: a machine that uses oil, coal, wind or waves to make electricity.

global warming: the build-up of heat within the earth's atmosphere. It affects the world's weather. Many scientists believe that global warming is melting the icecaps in the polar regions.

hemisphere: the top half or the bottom half of the earth.

hurricane: a dangerous tropical storm.

insulators: materials that do not allow heat to pass through easily.

medieval: a period in history, from around AD 1000 to AD 1500.

meteorologist: a scientist who studies the weather.

orbit: the path of a planet, moon or satellite in space.

Number work answers

page 6: The difference between 34.4°C (94°F) and -57.8°C (-72°F) is 92.2°C (166°F).
The difference between 57.8°C (136°F) and -89.2°C (-128.6°C) is 147°C (264.6°F).

Glossary

pollution: unwanted or waste material that makes air, water, buildings or land dirty. Noise and light can also cause pollution.

predict: to guess what will happen before it takes place.

radar: equipment which uses radio waves to find distant objects. It sends out radio waves and then records them as they bounce back. Radar can detect rain clouds.

satellite: a spacecraft containing scientific equipment that orbits the earth to record and send back information. Satellites record information about space and the weather on earth.

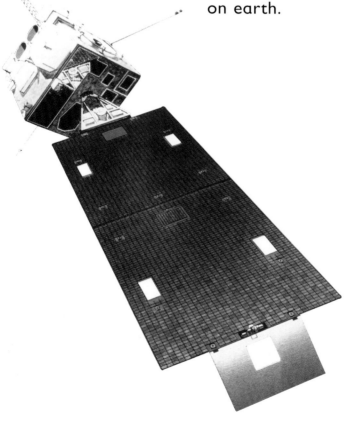

Scandinavian: from Scandinavia – the countries of Norway, Sweden, Denmark and Finland in Northern Europe.

seasons: changing weather patterns that happen at the same time each year.

subtropical: describes regions bordering the tropics where it is hot and fairly wet, with long, dry seasons.

temperate: a region in the world that has temperatures that are never very hot or very cold.

tornado: a violent whirlwind.

tropical: describes regions close to the equator (an imaginary line round the middle of the earth) that have a hot and wet climate.

water vapour: water when it is a gas. Water turns from a liquid to a gas when it is heated.

waterlogged: covered with, and full of, water.

weather: the day-to-day changes in rain, sunshine, temperature and wind.

weather stations: equipment used to store information about the weather. A weather station may be fixed, such as equipment stored in buildings or fields, or moving, such as satellites or balloons.

Index